Instant Poetry Frames
Around the Year

by Betsy Franco

NEW YORK • TORONTO • LONDON • AUCKLAND • SYDNEY
MEXICO CITY • NEW DELHI • HONG KONG • BUENOS AIRES

SCHOLASTIC
Teaching
Resources

To Joanie, who helps me with my writing all year long

Cover design by Jason Robinson
Cover and interior artwork by Maxie Chambliss
Interior design by Solutions by Design Inc.

ISBN: 0-439-59855-9

7 8 9 10   40   10 09 08 07

Contents

POETRY FRAMES

September

October

November

December

January

February

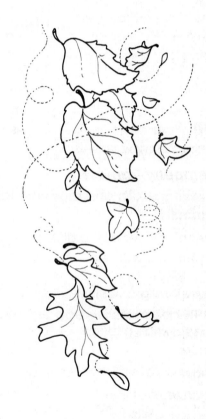

All year round, children can be successful, creative poets. The simple frames and starters in this book are designed to enable them to leap into poetry with confidence. The poetry frames are organized by month, from September to June, around themes students can relate to. By the end of the school year, children will end up with a poetry collection of their own that they can reread with pride.

What are poetry frames?

Poetry frames are quick and easy reproducible "invitations" into the world of poetry. They are simple, unfinished poems that invite students to complete them. Some have missing words; others have missing phrases. Some consist of blank lines with helpful questions and tips. All of the frames included in this collection give children the comfort of writing within a structure. They provide visual clues to help young poets brainstorm ideas and illustrate their own poetry.

Why use poetry frames?

To build writing skills and meet the language arts standards.

Confidence makes all the difference when a child is writing poetry. The structure of poetry frames gives students the support they need while developing a wide range of writing skills. Frames motivate young poets not only to write, but to keep writing! Using them helps children to:

- Write in a variety of poetry genres
- Organize their ideas
- Sequence events
- Use pictures to describe text
- Focus on specific parts of speech
- Apply mechanical conventions to their writing
- Write for a variety of purposes (to entertain, inform, explain, and describe)
- Edit and "publish" their work
- Use prewriting strategies to plan written work
- And much more!

To present a variety of poetry forms.

This collection includes a number of formal and informal poetic forms. It includes list poems, riddles, a number of visual (or concrete) poems, acrostic poetry, and a variation on the diamante. There are also two-word poems, poems that give directions, poems with questions, and collaborative poems.

To individualize instruction.

The different frames require varying degrees of participation from students. Some ask children to fill in words, and others invite them to write an entire poem. This variation allows you to individualize instruction because it enables everyone to participate at his or her own level.

To encourage self-expression.

Using poetry frames enables students to share their preferences, their opinions, and their feelings about familiar aspects of their world. Children are, for example, encouraged to introduce themselves, write about their feelings during the first and last weeks of school, and record their Halloween candy preferences. The frames also ask students to write about parents, family memories, and friends. These prompts encourage children to play with words and use their imaginations as they express themselves.

To introduce the basic elements of poetry.

Elements of poetic language are purposely interwoven throughout this book. Examples of similes, metaphors, personification, alliteration, and onomatopoeia are included. Students are invited to use zippy action words and describing words to paint a picture with their language. Children are also encouraged to play with different parts of speech—naming words (nouns), describing words (adjectives), and action words (verbs).

To build awareness of rhyme and rhythm.

Poetry frames are simply poems that need to be finished. They are structured so that they will be fun to write and to read aloud when completed. They often have a pattern of a repeated phrase, or rhyming couplets or quatrains to begin and end poems. Some poems rhyme throughout, but in most cases, children don't have to worry about the rhyming—they can just enjoy it. In a few cases, a list of helpful rhyming words for students to use is supplied.

To integrate math, science, and social studies into your language arts curriculum.

Poetry can so easily embrace the rest of the curriculum. In this collection, the frame "Thoughts for the 100th Day" touches on math. "Animals in the Arctic," "It's Great to Hibernate," "Baby Animals," "Butterfly Cycle," "Garden Bugs," and "A Trip to the Zoo" all involve science subjects, as do many weather and seasonal poems. "Proud on Presidents' Day" and other poetry frames about holidays and families certainly fit into the social studies curriculum.

Using the Frames in Your Classroom

Each poem can be written individually, with partners, or as a class collaboration. Here's how you might use the frames with children:

1. Make a copy of the frame of your choice for each student. Introduce the frame with the group before children begin. Review the directions together and write an example as a class.

2. Provide students with a copy of the reproducible frame and have them use pencil and crayons or markers to fill it in.

3. Circulate around the room to check that each child is engaged, helping to brainstorm when needed.

After poems are completed, celebrate kids' efforts by inviting them to:

* share with a partner or a small group
* read to the class or to an older buddy
* copy their poems onto blank sheets of paper and illustrate them as part of a display
* complete frames in a literacy center
* make their poems into a class collaborative book for the classroom library
* display poems on bulletin boards
* take home and share poems with families
* make poems into pocket chart strips (Poems can be written on blank strips and then displayed and chanted by the class.)
* act out the poems
* create their very own anthologies by binding all their poems together
* hold a poetry reading in which each child reads his or her poem to the whole class

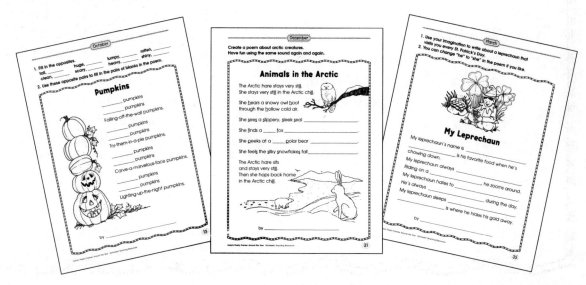

Poetry Frames

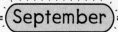

1. **Write a poem introducing yourself.**
2. **Then draw a picture of yourself.**

Introducing Me

My name is _____.

I'm in _____ grade.

In school, I think _____ is really great.

I love to _____,

I _____ with my friends.

I _____.

Well, that's me!

The end.

by _____

Write a poem as if you're writing in a journal.
Tell about your feelings in the first week of school.
You can use some of the words in the box if
you like.

excited	mad
sad	happy
surprised	glad
scared	hopeful

Dear Journal,

I just started school for the year.

I have lots of feelings.

Would you like to hear?

I feel _____

I feel _____.

I feel _____.

I feel _____.

Just look at all the feelings

I've already had—_____, _____, _____,
                          (Write some of your feelings.)
and glad.

Signed,

_____

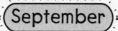
1. **Write a riddle about something in the classroom.**
2. **Give at least three clues.**

Example:

One end of me is soft and pink.
One end is sharp as a nail.
If you press me on a paper,
I leave a written trail.
What am I?

You can write about one of the items in the box, or about something else.
Your riddle doesn't have to rhyme.
Ask a friend to guess what you wrote about.

paper	markers
books	rulers
scissors	ball
chair	flag

Classroom Riddle

_____

_____

_____

_____

_____

What am I?

by _____

1. Fill in the first two blanks in the poem with describing words.
   What kinds of leaves do you see in the fall?

2. Fill in the last five blanks with action words.
   What can you do when you play in the leaves?

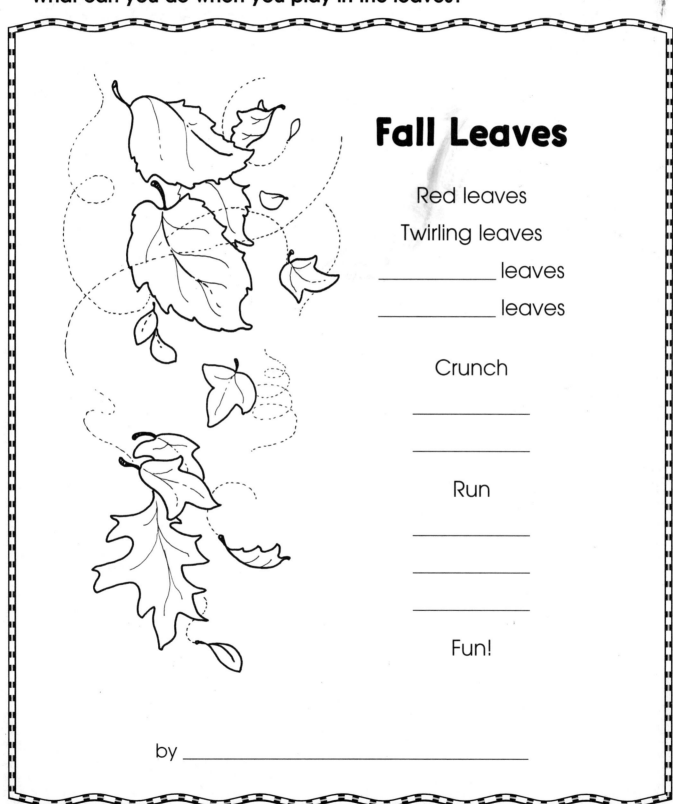

Fall Leaves

Red leaves

Twirling leaves

_____ leaves

_____ leaves

Crunch

_____

_____

Run

_____

_____

_____

Fun!

by _____

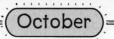

1. **Think about the ways children get to school on wheels. Here are some ideas:**

2. **Write a phrase on each spoke of the wheel.**

skateboard	car	bus
bike	scooter	truck

3. **Write the sound that each one makes. Or write what each one does.**

   Examples: *Skateboards* clackity-clack.
                   Scooters glide.

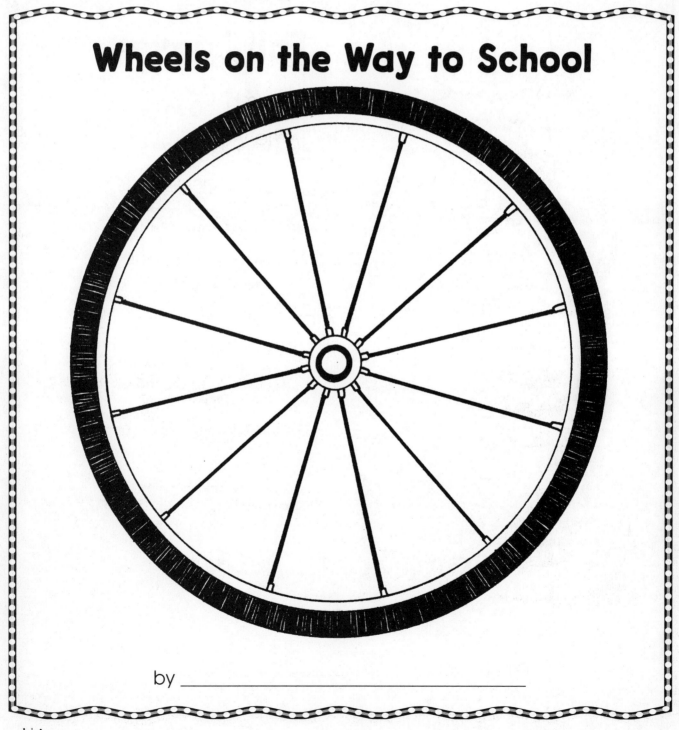

Wheels on the Way to School

by _____

Instant Poetry Frames: Around the Year Scholastic Teaching Resources

1. Fill in the opposites.

tall, _____   huge, _____   lumpy, _____   rotten, _____

clean, _____   scary, _____   heavy, _____   shiny, _____

2. Use these opposite pairs to fill in the pairs of blanks in the poem.

Pumpkins

_____ pumpkins

_____ pumpkins

Falling-off-the-wall pumpkins.

_____ pumpkins

_____ pumpkins

Try-them-in-a-pie pumpkins.

_____ pumpkins

_____ pumpkins

Carve-a-marvelous-face pumpkins.

_____ pumpkins

_____ pumpkins

Lighting-up-the-night pumpkins.

by _____

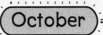

October is apple-gathering time. Describe what it's like to eat your favorite apple. You might think about questions like these to help you:

What does your favorite apple look like? What color is it?

How does it feel in your hands?

How does it smell?

How does it sound when you bite into it?

What does it taste like?

How do you feel after you eat it?

Apple Time Treat

My favorite apple _____

_____.

It _____

_____.

It _____

_____.

It _____

_____.

_____

_____

by _____

1. **Describe the Halloween treats you like and don't like.**

2. **For each line of the poem, use only two words.**

   Example: *chewy caramels*
   rainbow jellybeans

3. **Don't use the brand names of candies. Describe them!**

Sorting Treats on Halloween

Treats I Like:

_____ _____

_____ _____

_____ _____

_____ _____

Treats I Don't Like:

_____ _____

_____ _____

_____ _____

_____ _____

But it all works out on Halloween.

We trade back and forth for what we like to eat.

by _____

What are you thankful for?

1. Write a word or a phrase that starts with **each letter of** *thankful.*

   Example: *Turkey that makes my stomach purr*

2. Draw a picture of one of the things you're thankful for.

Thankful on Thanksgiving

T _____

H _____

A _____

N _____

K _____

F _____

U _____

L _____

by _____

Instant Poetry Frames: Around the Year Scholastic Teaching Resources

Thanksgiving is a time for families. Write about some of the things you remember about your family. Your memories can be funny, fun, sad, happy, angry, and wonderful.

My Family

I remember when _____

_____.

I remember when _____

_____.

I remember when _____

_____.

I remember when _____

_____.

I remember when _____

_____.

by _____

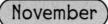

It's fun to make up words to use in a poem.

1. Finish this poem about getting sick.

2. Make up some words of your own.

   Examples: *googly-boogly*
   burpy-lurpy
   tangly-wangly

When I Get Sick

When I get sick,

my brain is hot.

It feels all _____.

My eyes feel very _____.

and my stomach is _____.

My hair is _____.

My nose is _____.

But then one morning,

with a *zippity-boom,*

I feel all better

and dash from my room!

by _____

Instant Poetry Frames: Around the Year Scholastic Teaching Resources

Fill in the blanks with action words to make two different poems.
You can use the action words in the box if you like.

Action Words:

stomp	hide	shake	tromp	quiver
weave	gobble	rip	skip	curl

Cold Winter Winds

The cold winds _____ into my bones.

I _____ and shiver.

My hands _____ inside my gloves.

I _____ through the snow to get back home.

Soon I'll _____ in my quilt and I won't be alone.

Cold Winter Winds

The cold winds _____ into my bones.

I _____ and shiver.

My hands _____ inside my gloves.

I _____ through the snow to get back home.

Soon I'll _____ in my quilt and I won't be alone.

by _____

Which poem do you like better? Put a star next to it.

A list poem is a poem with a list.

1. **Fill in the blanks to finish the silly poem below.**
   List all kinds of things in your bedroom.

2. **Draw a picture of something in your room covered in snow.**

If It Snowed Inside My Bedroom

If the roof came off

on a winter night,

my _____,

my _____,

and my _____

would be white.

My _____

and my _____

would make a silly white sight.

My _____

and my _____

would be white and bright.

If the roof came off

and it snowed that night,

my room would become

a white delight.

by _____

Instant Poetry Frames: Around the Year Scholastic Teaching Resources

Create a poem about arctic creatures.
Have fun using the same sound again and again.

Animals in the Arctic

The Arctic hare stays very still.
She stays very still in the Arctic chill.

She hears a snowy owl hoot
through the hollow cold air.

She sees a slippery, sleek seal _____.

She finds a _____ fox _____.

She peeks at a _____ polar bear _____.

She feels the silky snowflakes fall_____.

The Arctic hare sits
and stays very still.
Then she hops back home
in the Arctic chill.

by _____

What is one of your favorite books?

1. Write its title on the book
   on the right.

2. Then fill in the blanks below
   to finish the poem.

Use the questions below to help you.

Questions:

What do you love to do outdoors?

What is your favorite sport?

What food tastes delicious to you?

What is a cozy thing for you to do?

What is something you look forward to doing?

My Favorite Book

Reading my favorite book
is like drinking hot cocoa
on a winter night.

It's like _____.

It's like _____.

It's like _____.

It's out of sight!

by _____

Instant Poetry Frames: Around the Year Scholastic Teaching Resources

1. Imagine you are different animals hibernating.
2. Then fill in the blanks to finish the poem.

It's Great to Hibernate

If I were a bear,

I'd _____ .

If I were a frog,
I'd snuggle in the mud at the bottom of a lake.

If I were a chipmunk,

I'd _____ .

I'd _____ .
if I were a snake.

If I were a squirrel, I'd _____

_____ tree.

But I'm not a wild animal as you can see,
so my bed is the hibernating spot for me.

On nights when the snow
is thick and deep,
I curl up in my blanket cave
and close my eyes and fall asleep.

by _____

**In this poem, the mitten seems like it's alive. Finish the poem.
What would a mitten say?**

I'm Your Warm Winter Mitten

I'm your warm winter mitten,
all woolly and white.

I get into lots of snowball _____.

I help you _____

_____.

I help you _____

_____.

I cover your _____

and I _____.

And when the day's over,
you toss me about.
Then I finally have time
to rest and dry out.

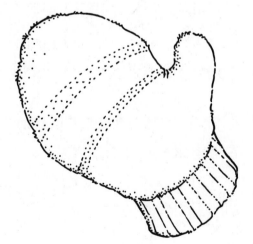

by _____

Instant Poetry Frames: Around the Year Scholastic Teaching Resources

1. **Write about a snowflake.**
2. **On each blank line, compare the snowflake to something else.**
   Example: *A snowflake is as soft as a baby's blanket.*

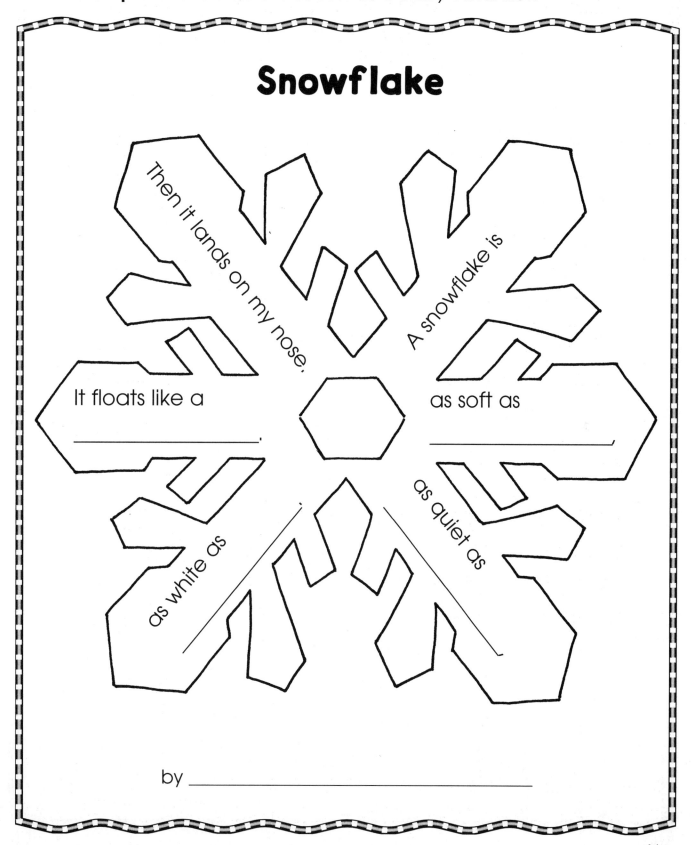

Snowflake

Then it lands on my nose.

A snowflake is

It floats like a
_____.

as soft as
_____

as white as
_____

as quiet as
_____

by _____

Martin Luther King, Jr., had strong beliefs and stood up for what he believed in.

Write a poem about someone who you think is strong.

You can use the words in the box to help you, or use words of your own.

| strong | brave | giving |
| wise | caring | smart |

On Martin Luther King, Jr., Day

Write the person's name.

Write words that describe the person.

Write what that person did.

Write words that describe the person.

Write a naming word for the person.

Examples: *peacemaker*
guide

by _____

Instant Poetry Frames: Around the Year Scholastic Teaching Resources

Use words that paint a picture to finish the snow poem.

Example: *We whizz down slick slopes on our battered sled.*

Fresh Snow

Whenever the snow is fresh and deep,

We wouldn't dare waste our time asleep.

We _____.

We _____.

We _____.

We _____.

It might turn slushy or melt away.

So when fresh snow falls, we're in it all day.

by _____

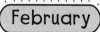

1. **Think about the number 100 on the 100th Day of School.**
2. **Fill in each pair of blanks with the name of an animal and an exciting adjective to describe the animal, like *stampeding zebras*.**

Thoughts for the 100th Day of School

100 _____ _____ would be friendlier

than 100 _____ _____.

100 _____ _____ would be cleaner

than 100 mud-caked hogs.

100 _____ _____ would be prettier

than 100 _____ _____.

100 _____ _____ would be quieter

than 100 ribbiting frogs.

100 _____ _____ would be _____

than 100 _____ _____.

100 _____ _____ would be wilder

than 100 miniature dogs!

Instant Poetry Frames: Around the Year Scholastic Teaching Resources

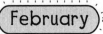

1. **Look up information to finish this poem.**
2. **Fill in the blanks with what you find.**

Proud on Presidents' Day

I'm proud of my country in so many ways.

My country's initials are ____. ____. ____.

I'm proud of my flag.

It's _____.

It hangs in the classroom every day.

I'm proud of my state.

Its flower is a _____.

Its bird is a _____.

The _____ is its tree.

My state of _____ is special to me.

I'm proud of the presidents we celebrate.

_____ and _____

were both first rate.

by _____

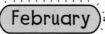

1. Use your imagination to write a Valentine poem about love.
2. Decorate your valentine.

Love—Valentine's Day

Love is the color _____.

Love smells like a loaf of warm rye bread.

Love sounds like _____.

Love tastes like _____.

Love looks like _____.

Love feels like _____.

by _____

Instant Poetry Frames: Around the Year Scholastic Teaching Resources

1. **Think about a friend.**
2. **Write a poem about how you and your friend are like magnets that stick together.**

   Your friend can be:

a classmate	a pet	a brother or sister
a cousin	a neighbor	someone else

_____ and I Are Magnets

(Fill in your friend's name.)

_____ and I are magnets.

We like to _____ together.

We like to _____ together.

We always _____ together.

And we always _____ together.

_____ and I are magnets.

We always stick together.

No matter where we are,

how we're feeling, or the weather!

by _____

1. **Write about how spring chases winter away.**
2. **Fill in the blanks to show the change in the weather.**

Scat, Winter

"Scat, winter.

It's my turn,"

said Spring.

"Take away your _____.

I'm here with my _____.

Take away your _____.

I'm here with my _____.

Take away your _____.

I'm here with my _____.

Take away your _____.

I'm here with my _____."

"Scat, winter.

Time to pack.

But don't be sad.

You'll soon be back."

by _____

Instant Poetry Frames: Around the Year Scholastic Teaching Resources

Use the questions below to help you write a poem with sound effects.

You can use the words in the box to help you, or use words of your own.

drip	plop	drop
splash	ping	ting

Questions: *How does rain sound...*
on a window pane?
on the roof of a car?
in a puddle?

Rainy-Day Sound Effects

Plink, plink, plinkity-plunk.

Rain plinks in the empty metal bucket.

_____ .

Rain _____ .

_____ .

Rain _____ .

_____ .

Rain _____ .

_____ .

by _____

1. **Close your eyes and picture what the wind does.**
2. **Finish this poem about the wind.**

The Spring Wind Can't, The Spring Wind Can

The wind can't lift my school,

but it can topple over a chair.

The wind can't move a tree,

but it can _____.

The wind can't empty a lake,

but it can _____.

The wind can't pull off my coat,

but it can _____.

The wind can't _____,

but it can _____.

The wind can't be seen

as it whirls through the air.

But the wind has lots of ways

to show it's there.

by _____

1. **Use your imagination to write about a leprechaun that visits you every St. Patrick's Day.**
2. **You can change "he" to "she" in the poem if you like.**

My Leprechaun

My leprechaun's name is _____.

_____ is his favorite food when he's chowing down.

My leprechaun always _____.

Riding on a _____, he zooms around.

My leprechaun hates to _____.

He's always _____ during the day.

My leprechaun sleeps _____.

_____ is where he hides his gold away.

by _____

Fill in the blanks to write a poem about spring fever.
How does spring fever make you feel?
> **Example:** *I feel like racing a dragonfly.*

Spring Fever

Whenever the weather
begins to get springy,
I get spring fever.
I'm wild and dingy!

I feel like _____.
I feel like jumping up over the sun.

I feel like _____.
I feel like petting a bee for fun.

I feel like _____.
I feel like leaping as far as a frog.

I feel like _____.
I feel like howling like a puppy dog.

Whenever it's spring,
I'm wild. I'm free.
Spring fever takes over,
and you can't stop me!

by _____

1. **Give directions for having fun inside on a rainy day.**
2. **Let the pictures help you think of ideas.**

Inside Fun on a Drippy Day

If you're inside on a drippy day,
use your imagination—it'll be okay.
Invite some friends and play, play, play,
even if the sky is gray.

First, _____.

Next, _____.

Next, _____.

Then, _____.

Don't forget to _____.

Finish off by _____.

Even if the rain won't go away,
A drippy day can be A-Okay!

by _____

Ask questions about baby animals in the spring.

Example: *Do baby rabbits have pink twitchy noses?*

Baby Animals

Do baby bees _____?

Do baby birds _____?

Are there sticky trails behind baby snails?

Do baby turtles _____?

Do baby frogs _____?

Do baby gators have skin with scales?

Do baby _____?

Do baby _____?

Do baby squirrels have bushy tails?

I'm curious about babies in the spring
and I wish I knew most everything
about tails and eyes and shells and wings
and all sorts of other interesting things.

by _____

A kite pulses like a jellyfish or a heartbeat. What else is a kite like? Write in the blanks to finish the poem.

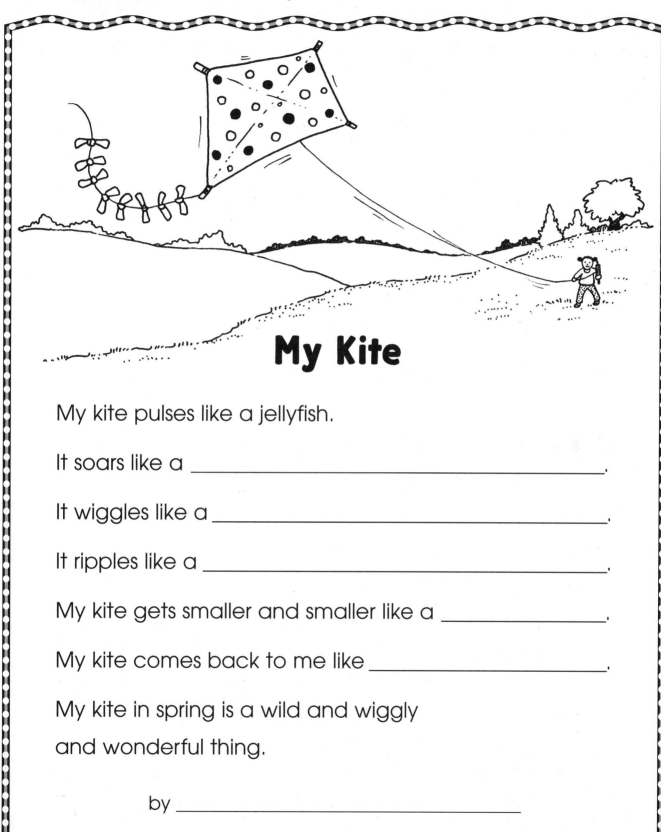

My Kite

My kite pulses like a jellyfish.

It soars like a _____.

It wiggles like a _____.

It ripples like a _____.

My kite gets smaller and smaller like a _____.

My kite comes back to me like _____.

My kite in spring is a wild and wiggly

and wonderful thing.

by _____

1. Create a poem in a circle.
2. Write about the four stages of a butterfly—egg,
   caterpillar, pupa inside a chrysalis, and butterfly!

Butterfly Cycle

1

Egg

Itty-bitty, teeny-weeny.
You have to squint to
even see me.
When I hatch,
I wonder what I'll be.

Caterpillar

_____

_____

_____

When I change,
I wonder what I'll be.

2

4

Butterfly

_____

_____

_____

A butterfly in flight!
That's what I'll be!

Pupa in a Chrysalis

_____

_____

_____

When I change,
I wonder what
I'll be.

3

by _____

Instant Poetry Frames: Around the Year   Scholastic Teaching Resources

1. To write a Mother's Day poem, fill in the short blanks with the word *mother*, *grandmother*, or the name of another person who is a mother to you.

2. Don't forget to give your poem a title.
   Example: *Mrs. Sacks*

3. Then fill in the long blanks.

My _____
(Fill in the name.)

_____ always says _____.

_____ would tell you I'm _____.

_____ helps me _____.

_____ and I like to _____.

_____ can't stand it when I _____.

_____ loves it when I _____.

And now that Mother's Day is here,

_____ deserves a great big cheer!

by _____

Use the pictures to help you write about puddles.

Puddles Are for...

_____

_____

_____

_____

_____

But most of all,

puddles are for

_____!

by _____

Instant Poetry Frames: Around the Year   Scholastic Teaching Resources

Use these rhyming words and others to write a garden poem.

Write about the bugs in the garden—snails, slugs, butterflies, bees.

Rhyme every two lines. Have fun!

snail	slug	butterfly	bee
trail	ugh	shy	tree
pale	bug	why	me
fail	snug	sky	flee
pail	tug	good-bye	see
tale	hug	by	three
tail	shrug	passerby	agree

Garden Bugs

In my garden, the shy little snail _____

_____.

In my garden, _____

_____.

In my garden, _____

_____.

In my garden, _____

_____.

Snails, slugs, butterflies, bees!

There's almost no room left for me.

by _____

Write a group poem with other children.

1. Write what you think dads do best on the first two blanks.
2. Then ask other children what dads do best.
3. Write their answers on the other blanks.

What Dads Do Best

Dads _____

_____.

Dads _____

_____.

Dads _____

_____.

Dads _____

_____.

Dads _____

_____.

Dads _____

_____.

It's Father's Day—I'll bet you guessed.
Let's tell the dads what they do best!

by _____

Instant Poetry Frames: Around the Year Scholastic Teaching Resources

1. **Fill in the blanks with zippy action words and describing words.**

   Example: *I gobbled up*
   drippy spoonfuls
   of sticky fruit salad.

2. **Use the words in the box or others you make up.**

juicy	gnawed	drippy
chomped	bit	raw
slurpy	gobbled	crunched
munched	gulped	tasty

My Favorite Picnic Food

I <u>crunched</u>

a fistful of crisp ruffly potato chips.

I _____

some _____ carrots and celery.

I _____

some _____ barbecued chicken.

I _____

a sliver of _____ watermelon.

And the frosting on the cake
was great for lickin'.
Yum!

by _____

1. **Find the pattern in this poem.**
2. **Then fill in the blanks.**

A Trip to the Zoo

A cheetah's made for running.

A monkey's made for _____ .

A lion's made for _____ .

A _____'s made for _____ .

A _____ .

A _____ .

A _____ .

A _____ .

A _____ .

Someday I'll set free
the animals in the zoo
so they can do
what they're made to do.

by _____

Write about what you'll miss and what you won't miss when school is over.

When School's Over

I won't miss _____.

I won't miss _____.

I won't miss _____.

I won't miss _____.

I will miss _____.

I will miss _____.

I will miss _____.

I will miss _____.

Summer will be fun for one and all.

See you at school when it turns to fall!

by _____

Notes

_____

_____

_____

_____

_____

_____

_____

_____

_____

_____

_____

_____

Instant Poetry Frames: Around the Year Scholastic Teaching Resources